©2024, Frank Young

# Pandas, China, and the World

A Short Up-and-Down History of Pandas as a Part of China's Diplomacy

# Frank Young

Poplar House Press, 2024

# Preface

In the realm of international diplomacy, where the stakes are high and tensions often run deep, one unlikely ambassador has captured the hearts and imaginations of people around the world: the panda. With its endearing black-and-white fur and gentle demeanor, the panda has transcended its status as a mere symbol of China's rich biodiversity to become an icon of peace, friendship, and cooperation on the global stage.

In "Pandas, China, and the World: A Short Up-and-Down History of Pandas as a Part of China's Diplomacy," we embark on a captivating journey through the intricate web of panda diplomacy. From the early days of gifting pandas as symbols of goodwill to foreign nations to the modern era of panda loans and conservation efforts, this book explores the multifaceted role that pandas have played in China's diplomatic endeavors.

Through meticulous research and insightful analysis, we uncover the fascinating stories behind some of the most significant moments in panda diplomacy. From the historic visit of U.S. President Richard Nixon to China in 1972, which paved the way for the iconic arrival of Ling-Ling and Hsing-Hsing at the National Zoo in Washington, D.C., to the more recent panda loans extended during major international events such as Beijing Olympics, each chapter offers a nuanced perspective on the evolving relationship between pandas, China, and the world.

But this is not merely a recounting of diplomatic exchanges and political maneuvering. It is also a celebration of the enduring appeal of these beloved creatures and the universal values they represent: friendship, cooperation, and a shared commitment to conservation and environmental stewardship.

As we delve into the ups and downs of panda diplomacy, we invite readers to ponder the profound significance of these bamboo-munching ambassadors and their role in shaping the course of history. For in the story of pandas, China, and the world, we find not only a reflection of our past but also a beacon of hope for a future built on understanding, respect, and harmony.

So, join us as we embark on this extraordinary journey, where the fate of nations hangs in the balance and where pandas reign supreme as symbols of diplomacy, unity, and peace.

Frank Young
West Windsor, New Jersey
February, 2024

# Outline of Content

Our journey begins with an exploration of "Some Facts About Pandas," delving into the physical characteristics and endearing behaviors that have made these pandas beloved worldwide. From there, we traverse through the ever-evolving landscape of "Panda News in Contemporary Media," where the portrayal of pandas shapes public perception and diplomatic relations. We then embark onto the rich history of "Pandas as Gifts in Chinese Diplomacy," uncovering the intricate dance of diplomacy and conservation that has characterized panda exchanges between nations. Our path leads us to the historic exchange between "Pandas, Madame Nixon, Madame Mao, and Premier Zhou Enlai," shedding light on the pivotal role of these bears played in fostering international goodwill. We then take our readers to "Pandas as Diplomatic Gifts and Chinese Media", "Stories About Ling-Ling and Hsing-Hsing in Chinese Media", and "Roles of Pandas Told in Chinese Media" to share with our readers what are highlighted and made aware of in the Chinese media. As we journey on, we witness the global impact of "Loaning Pandas to Various Zoos of Note," where pandas serve as ambassadors for conservation and cultural exchange. However, our exploration also confronts the challenges of "Events of Diplomatic Recalls of Pandas," revealing the vulnerabilities of panda diplomacy to political tensions. Yet, amidst the complexities, we find hope in "The World as a Whole in Helping Pandas," recognizing the collective effort required to ensure the survival of these treasured creatures. Ultimately, we conclude with a resounding call to action: "Panda is World's Treasure and Should not be Used as a Political Tool," urging for a renewed commitment to protect pandas from the vagaries of diplomacy and preserve them for future generations.

# Some Facts About Pandas

The panda, formally known as the giant panda (Ailuropoda melanoleuca), is believed to have existed as a distinct species for millions of years, but its evolutionary history is complex. The fossil record indicates that ancestors of the panda diverged from other bears around 18 to 22 million years ago during the late Miocene epoch.

However, the modern panda as we know it likely emerged as a distinct species more recently. Based on genetic evidence, researchers estimate that panda's lineage diverged from other bears around 4 to 5 million years ago during the Pliocene epoch. This suggests that pandas have been a distinct species for several million years.

Despite their long evolutionary history, pandas have faced significant challenges in recent centuries, including habitat loss, fragmentation, and poaching, leading to their classification as an endangered species. Conservation efforts are ongoing to protect and preserve these iconic animals and their habitats for future generations.

Pandas are native to the mountainous regions of central China, primarily inhabiting the bamboo forests of Sichuan, Shaanxi, and Gansu provinces. These areas are characterized by dense bamboo thickets, cool temperatures, and rugged terrain. Pandas are most commonly found at elevations between 1,200 and 3,400 meters (3,900 to 11,100 feet) above sea level.

Within their habitat, pandas establish home ranges that can span several square kilometers, with males having larger ranges than females. They rely on bamboo forests for food and shelter, as bamboo makes up the majority of their diet. Additionally, these mountainous regions provide pandas with protection from predators and ample opportunities for denning and breeding.

Conservation efforts in China and around the world focus on preserving and restoring the natural habitats of pandas, including the protection of bamboo forests and the establishment of wildlife reserves and corridors to connect fragmented panda populations.

Here are some more interesting and distinguishing characteristics and facts about pandas:

1. **Endangered species**: Classified as endangered, there are about 1,800 pandas remaining in the wild. Their primary threats include habitat loss due to deforestation and fragmentation, as well as poaching.

2. **Distinctive appearance**: Pandas are easily recognizable by their distinctive black-and-white fur patterns. This coloration helps them blend into their bamboo forest habitat.

3. **Bamboo diet**: Pandas are primarily herbivores, with bamboo making up 99% of their diet. They have evolved a special thumb-like extension of the wrist bone, which helps them grasp bamboo stalks and strip off the leaves.

4. **Solitary animals**: Pandas are generally solitary animals, spending most of their time foraging for food. They have large home ranges and communicate through vocalizations and scent marking.

5. **Low reproductive rate**: Pandas have a relatively low reproductive rate. Female pandas are fertile for only a few days each year, making successful mating and breeding in captivity a challenge.

6. **Cultural symbol**: Pandas hold significant cultural importance, particularly in China, where they are considered national treasures and symbols of conservation efforts. They are often featured in Chinese art, folklore, and international diplomacy, as detailed in this book.

7. **Adaptations for cold climate**: Pandas have several adaptations to cope with their cold, mountainous habitat, including thick fur coats and a low metabolic rate to conserve energy.

8.  **Excellent climbers**: Despite their large size, pandas are skilled climbers and are capable of climbing trees to forage for food or escape predators.

9.  **Global icon**: Pandas are beloved around the world and are often featured in conservation campaigns, zoos, and wildlife documentaries. Their charismatic appearance and gentle demeanor make them one of the most popular and recognizable animals.

10.  **Lifespan**: The lifespan of a panda, both in the wild and in captivity, typically ranges from 20 to 30 years. However, pandas in the wild often have shorter lifespans due to various factors such as predation, habitat loss, and limited access to medical care. In captivity, where pandas receive specialized care, proper nutrition, and medical attention, they tend to live longer lives. The oldest known giant panda in captivity lived to be over 38 years old.

# Panda News in Contemporary Media

History of pandas in the United States is long and touchy. However, recently, the media are filled with news about this lovely animal that "they would all leave the country, for good." Here are a few such reports as samples.

**"Say goodbye to the pandas: All black-and-white bears on US soil set to return to China**

There will soon be no pandas in the U.S. for the first time since 1972, after U.S. zoos' agreements with China are set to expire by the end of next year.... The move comes as zoos in Memphis, Atlanta, and San Diego have already returned their pandas or are going to by the end of the year, marking the first time in 50 years the U.S. will not have any pandas", reported by Zoe Well, USA TODAY, September 29, 2023.

**"All pandas in U.S. zoos are heading back to China, threatening five decades of "Panda Diplomacy"**

The three giant pandas at the Smithsonian's National Zoo in Washington, D.C., are returning to China. Soon, there may not be any pandas in American zoos. Rising tensions between the two superpowers may threaten one of the most popular attractions at American zoos", according to the CBS News National Correspondent Adriana Diaz, November 8, 2023.

**"Bye-bye, pandas: Amid curdling U.S.-China relations, zoo loses beloved beasts after 51 years**

Pandas have been a symbolic barometer of U.S.-China ties. They're now a sign of trouble. For decades, they were cuddly emblems of global co-operation. Now, they're a bamboo-munching testament to a more turbulent world. Beloved giant pandas that came to define the zoo in the U.S. capital are gone. All three remaining ones were carted off Wednesday to the airport for a long flight to China. Thus ended 51 years of pandas at Washington's Smithsonian National Zoo, where their enclave was the geographic centre, the top draw and the heart of the zoo. Some of the final visitors to see its pandas choked back tears as they bid farewell to creatures they'd come to know by name", reported by Alexander Panetta, a Washington-based correspondent for CBC News, November 8, 2023.

**"The National Zoo's panda program is ending after more than 50 years as China looks elsewhere**

Three giant pandas left their enclosure at the Smithsonian National Zoo in Washington, DC, and departed by plane back to China on Wednesday, marking the end of more than 50 years of Chinese pandas being housed at the zoo.... Zoo staff call it a "hiatus" in their five-decade wildly popular panda program; Chinese officials have yet to say whether it will continue. And with relations between the two superpowers in a constant state of flux, these national treasures may be finding themselves part of the extension of the diplomatic chaos that has taken over the relationship between the two countries. The pandas' departure from the National Zoo leaves Zoo Atlanta as the only other US zoo to feature pandas from China, and not for much longer. The contracts for Atlanta's four bears expire next year, with no word on an extension", reported by Yong Xiong, Melissa Gray and David Culver, CNN correspondents, November 8, 2023.

It was, and still is, heart-broken for many panda-lovers to read such reports.

Then, this news came.

**"Take Heart, It Looks Like China Could Send New Pandas to the US**

Chinese President Xi Jinping is signaling that China will send new pandas to the United States.

SAN FRANCISCO (AP) — Chinese President Xi Jinping signaled that China will send new pandas to the United States, calling them 'envoys of friendship between the Chinese and American peoples.'", according to the Associated Press, November 16, 2023.

**"China promises pandas for the U.S. on the 45th anniversary of the two nations' ties**

BEIJING — Chinese Foreign Minister Wang Yi said Friday that the United States and China must insist on peaceful coexistence and transcend their differences like they did when they established diplomatic relations 45 years ago this week. Wang also promised that giant pandas would return to the U.S. — and specifically California — by the end of the year. `China-U.S. cooperation is no longer a dispensable option for the two countries or even for the world, but a must-answer question that must be seriously addressed,' he said", according to the Associated Press, January 5, 2024.

Really? Are you kidding me?

In fact, amidst the recent rollercoaster of panda news in the USA, it is worth remembering that this is just a tiny snapshot in the grand saga of panda diplomacy. From diplomatic gifts to international treaties, pandas have long been at the forefront of fostering goodwill between nations. So, while today's headlines may focus on the latest panda drama or dilemma, let's not forget the rich and complex history that precedes it. After all, pandas have been waddling through the corridors of diplomacy long before Twitter feeds and news tickers existed.

# Pandas as Gifts in Chinese Diplomacy

The tradition of giving pandas as diplomatic gifts from China dates back several decades, with the first recorded instance occurring in the heated wartime of World War II, involving Madame Chiang, the then First Lady of China, and David Crockett Graham, a legendary polymath American Baptist minister, who was also an archaeologist, anthropologist, naturalist, and field collector, residing then in Sichuan, from 1911 to 1948, enlisted by Madame Chiang to capture a live panda for the task.

The story of Madame Chiang enlisting David Crockett Graham to capture a live panda in the summer of 1941 is a fascinating tale that itself intertwines diplomacy, adventure, and the pursuit of exotic animals.

Madame Chiang Kai-shek, also known as Soong Mei-ling, was a prominent figure in Chinese politics and the wife of Generalissimo Chiang Kai-shek, the leader of the Republic of China during the tumultuous period of the mid-20th century. She was known for her strong personality and influence, both within China and internationally.

## Madame Chiang Kai-Shek (Soong Mei-Ling)

David Crockett Graham, an American naturalist and explorer, was living in China at the time and had developed a reputation for his adventurous spirit and expertise in capturing wild animals. Madame Chiang approached Graham with a unique task: to capture live pandas for diplomatic purposes.

In 1941, China was embroiled in the Second Sino-Japanese War, and Madame Chiang saw an opportunity to strengthen relations between China and the United States by gifting pandas as a symbol of goodwill. Pandas were rare and highly sought-after creatures, and obtaining them alive was no small feat.

Graham embarked on an expedition into the remote mountains of Sichuan Province, known as the natural habitat of giant pandas. Accompanied by local guides and equipped with little more than his wits and determination, Graham ventured deep into panda territory.

## David Crockett Graham

David Crockett Graham was an American mountaineer and explorer known for his pioneering expeditions in the Himalayas during the early 20th century. Born in 1884, Graham developed a passion for adventure from a young age, eventually leading him to explore the remote regions of Tibet and Nepal. He is remembered for his daring ascents of several unclimbed peaks, including the formidable Mount Kailash. Graham's remarkable feats and contributions to Himalayan exploration have left an enduring legacy in the mountaineering community, inspiring future generations of adventurers to push the boundaries of exploration and discovery.

After weeks of arduous trekking and careful observation, Graham and his team managed to locate and capture two live pandas. The capture itself would have been a remarkable achievement, given the elusive nature of pandas and the rugged terrain of their habitat.

The pandas were transported back to Graham's house in Chengdu, where they were cared for and acclimatized to captivity. Eventually, arrangements were made for their formal handover to a representative of the Bronx Zoo in Chongqing, the wartime capital of China.

The handover ceremony would have been a momentous occasion, symbolizing the friendship between China and the United States during a challenging period in history. The pandas' journey from the mountains of Sichuan to the Bronx Zoo in New York would have captured the imagination of people on both sides of the Pacific.

Overall, the story of Madame Chiang enlisting David Crockett Graham to capture live pandas in 1941 is a testament to the power of diplomacy, the allure of exotic animals, and the spirit of adventure that characterized the era, and might deserve a separate occasion to elaborate in details.

In 1949, the government of Republic of China moved to Taiwan and People's Republic of China was established under Mao Zedong's Chinese Communist Party (CCP). Below are a few notable moments in the history of panda diplomacy after 1949.

**1957**: China presented two pandas, Ping Ping and An An, to the Soviet Union in 1957, marking the beginning of modern panda diplomacy. These pandas were a gesture of friendship and cooperation between the two communist nations.

**1965**: Chinese leader Mao Zedong gifted a panda to North Korea (DPRK) for the first time in 1965. By 1980, at least five pandas were given to North Korea. North Korea was just the second country to receive pandas after the Soviet Union. However, on August 11, 2023, Yeji Chung of NK News published a report -

**"A mystery in black and white: The curious case of North Korea's missing pandas**

China has gifted more pandas to the DPRK than any other country, but the animal ambassadors haven't been seen for years."

**1972:** As a symbol of warming relations between the United States and China, China gifted two pandas, Ling-Ling and Hsing-Hsing, to the National Zoo in Washington, D.C. in 1972. This gesture came following President Richard Nixon's historic visit to China, which marked the normalization of relations between the two countries.

**1980-1990:** Throughout the 1980s and 1990s, China continued to use pandas as diplomatic gifts, exchanging them with various countries as a symbol of friendship and goodwill. Recipients include Japan, the United Kingdom, France, South Korea, Taiwan, and more.

**1984:** The United Kingdom received two pandas, Chia Chia and Ching Ching, from China in 1984 as part of the negotiations for the transfer of Hong Kong's sovereignty back to China. These pandas were housed at the London Zoo.

**Research and conservation efforts**: In addition to serving as diplomatic gifts, pandas have also been loaned to foreign countries for research and conservation purposes. These "panda loans" typically involve agreements where the recipient country pays a fee for the pandas' care, with any cubs born during the loan period considered property of China.

Overall, panda diplomacy has been a significant tool for China to strengthen diplomatic ties, promote cultural exchange, and raise awareness about conservation efforts for this endangered species.

Among the historical events, the one in 1972 is full of drama.

# Pandas, Madame Nixon, Madame Mao, and Premier Zhou Enlai

The story involving pandas, Madame Nixon, Madame Mao, and Premier Zhou Enlai in 1972 revolves around a significant moment in diplomatic history between the United States and China, which coincided with the visit of President Richard Nixon to China in February 1972, when China was still in its heat of the Great Proletarian Cultural Revolution.

During President Nixon's historic visit to China, which marked the first time a U.S. president had visited the People's Republic of China, there was a notable exchange involving pandas.

First, the story goes that, Madame Mao, also known as Jiang Qing, the wife of Chinese leader Mao Zedong, expressed to President Nixon's wife, Pat Nixon, her desire to present the United States with a pair of giant pandas as a gesture of goodwill. This gesture was seen as significant in the context of the warming relations between the two countries, which had been estranged for decades.

**President and Mrs. Nixon (Richard and Pat)**

Tian An Men (Gate of Heavenly Peace) in Beijing in 1970s

**Streets of Beijing in 1970s.**

## Madame Mao (Jiang Qing)

Here is another version of the story.

During the visit, President Nixon and his wife, First Lady Pat Nixon, met with Chinese Premier Zhou Enlai, one of the most influential figures in the Chinese Communist Party and a key architect of China's foreign policy. It was during this meeting that the topic of pandas arose.

Madame Nixon, known for her charm and grace, expressed her fondness for pandas to Premier Zhou Enlai, remarking that they were her favorite animal. Premier Zhou, recognizing the symbolic importance of the gesture, seized the opportunity to strengthen the budding diplomatic relationship between China and the United States.

In response to Madame Nixon's expressed interest, Premier Zhou offered to gift a pair of giant pandas to the United States as a symbol of friendship and goodwill. President Nixon and Madame Nixon graciously accepted the offer, recognizing the significance of the gesture in the context of improving Sino-American relations.

And, there is a third version of the story, which should not be missed to tell as well. Here you go.

According to this version, Madame Nixon visited Beijing Zoo right upon her arrival in the Chinese capital, just to see the pandas there, which she adored very much. This trip was reported to Premier Zhou Enlai quickly by his subordinates in charge of foreign affairs. Then at the farewell banquet held by Premier Zhou in honor of President Nixon and Madame Nixon, Premier Zhou subtly introduced the topic of pandas by pointing to a cigarette box adorned with a panda image. He straightforwardly asked Madame Nixon if she would like to have it, to which Madame Nixon, perhaps misunderstanding the question, replied that she did not smoke.

Premier Zhou, realizing the miscommunication, clarified that he was referring to the pandas themselves, not the cigarette box. Madame Nixon, upon understanding that Premier Zhou was offering pandas as a gift, became excited and immediately grasped the significance of the gesture.

In her enthusiasm, Madame Nixon jumped up and exclaimed to her husband, President Nixon, about the offer of pandas, saying: "Honey, they want to give pandas to us!", ignoring Premier Zhou in presence. She recognized the potential for the gift to symbolize the warming relations between the United States and China and eagerly embraced the opportunity to accept the pandas on behalf of the American people.

This version of the story adds a humorous and slightly more nuanced element to the exchange between Madame Nixon and Premier Zhou, emphasizing the cultural and linguistic differences that sometimes arise in diplomatic encounters. Despite the initial confusion, the ultimate result was the same: the pandas were gifted to the United States, becoming cherished symbols of friendship between the two nations.

More about this version of the story will be presented later as told by the Chinese media.

**Premier Zhou Enlai**

**Premier Zhou Enlai: "Would you like to have this?"**

The pandas chosen for this diplomatic exchange were two young pandas, a female named Ling-Ling and a male named Hsing-Hsing. The selection process involved careful consideration of various factors, including the pandas' health, temperament, and genetic diversity. Chinese officials aimed to choose pandas that would adapt well to their new environment in the United States and contribute to the conservation efforts for the species.

The actual logistics of transporting pandas to the United States, however, presented a real challenge, as giant pandas are rare and delicate animals. Through careful arrangement, Ling-Ling and Hsing-Hsing were then smoothly transported to the United States in April 1972 and made their new home at the National Zoo in Washington, D.C.

As the pandas made their debut at the National Zoo, crowds of eager spectators gathered to catch a glimpse of the majestic creatures. People from all walks of life, including families, schoolchildren, and dignitaries, flocked to the zoo.

The media frenzy surrounding Ling-Ling and Hsing-Hsing was unparalleled, with newspapers, magazines, and television stations providing extensive coverage of the pandas' arrival and their new life in America. Photographers jostled for the perfect shot, capturing images of the pandas exploring their new habitat and interacting with zookeepers.

Visitors to the National Zoo were treated to special exhibits and events celebrating the pandas' presence, including educational programs about panda conservation and Chinese culture. Merchandise featuring Ling-Ling and Hsing-Hsing, such as plush toys and souvenirs, flew off the shelves, further fueling the panda craze sweeping the nation.

The pandas quickly became beloved icons, symbolizing not only the burgeoning friendship between the United States and China but also the importance of wildlife conservation and international cooperation. Ling-Ling and Hsing-Hsing's endearing personalities and playful antics endeared them to people of all ages, leaving a lasting legacy that continues to this day.

Ling-Ling lived for 23 years (1969-1992) and Hsing-Hsing 29 years (1970-1999). During their time at the National Zoo, the pair had five cubs between 1983 and 1989, but they did not survive past a few days.

The story of pandas, Madame Nixon, Madame Mao, and Premier Zhou Enlai in 1972 is a poignant example of how animals can serve as ambassadors of diplomacy and friendship between nations, even during periods of great political tensions.

A Portrait of Ling-Ling and Hsing-Hsing

# Pandas as Diplomatic Gifts and Chinese Media

In the realm of Chinese media, the use of pandas as diplomatic gifts has long been a subject of both interest and scrutiny. These charismatic creatures, beloved by people worldwide, hold a special place in Chinese culture and diplomacy. When pandas are gifted to foreign countries, it often garners significant attention from Chinese media outlets, which closely monitor and analyze the implications of such gestures.

Chinese media coverage of panda diplomacy tends to emphasize the symbolic significance of these gestures, portraying them as expressions of China's desire for peaceful coexistence and friendship on the global stage. Reports often highlight the joy and excitement generated by the arrival of pandas in foreign countries, as well as the positive diplomatic outcomes that can result from such exchanges.

However, alongside the celebratory tone, Chinese media also engage in critical analysis of panda diplomacy, particularly regarding concerns about conservation and animal welfare. Some commentators raise questions about the ethical implications of keeping pandas in foreign zoos or breeding programs, expressing worries about the potential exploitation or commodification of these endangered species.

Moreover, Chinese media occasionally scrutinize the motives behind panda gifts, especially in cases where political tensions or controversies surround the receiving country. While pandas are intended to serve as symbols of friendship, their use in diplomacy can also be perceived as a form of political leverage or manipulation, prompting debates about the true nature of China's intentions.

Overall, Chinese media coverage of the use of pandas as diplomatic gifts reflects a complex blend of pride, skepticism, and pragmatism. While acknowledging the positive diplomatic outcomes that can result from panda diplomacy, media outlets also engage in nuanced discussions about the broader implications and ethical considerations associated with this practice.

In the following two sections, we describe in some detail the stories told in the Chinese media about the pandas Ling-Ling and Hsing-Hsing gifted through President and Mrs. Nixon and about the roles of pandas in the world which will be of separate interests for our readers.

# Stories About Ling-Ling and Hsing-Hsing in Chinese Media

Below we retell the stories told to the Chinese readers by some of the most popular Chinese media. Of course, the stories start from the visit of the Nixon couple.

In 1972, President Nixon visited China at the invitation of Premier Zhou Enlai, marking the first-ever visit by a sitting U.S. president to the country. Nixon's trip to China, famously known as the "Week That Changed the World," symbolized a significant breakthrough in Sino-American relations. While politicians may remember it for the details outlined in the Shanghai Communique, the public's memory of this historic diplomatic event is often associated with the pandas—Ling-Ling and Hsing-Hsing—gifted by China to the United States.

To understand this historical moment, we must begin with Nixon's advance team to China. Prior to Nixon's official visit, several advance groups led by senior government officials from the United States were dispatched to China. One notable aspect that left a deep impression, especially on Tang Longbin, the Director of Protocol at the Ministry of Foreign Affairs, was that almost every advance group made a mandatory stop at the panda pavilion in the Beijing Zoo. They even altered their itineraries, originally slated for visits to the Great Wall at Badaling, just to catch a glimpse of these beloved creatures. Initially, Tang Longbin didn't pay much attention to this, as he understood that while pandas were already renowned worldwide as China's national treasure, they remained a rare sight for foreigners, and their adorable demeanor was hard to resist.

**President and Mrs. Nixon arrive in Beijing and are greeted by Premier Zhou Enlai at the airport.**

On February 21, 1972, President Nixon, accompanied by his wife, arrived in China as scheduled. Mrs. Nixon, in particular, showed a keen interest in pandas. Despite several itinerary modifications, the visit to the zoo to see the pandas remained unchanged. Tang Longbin, who accompanied Mrs. Nixon, vividly recalls her excitement upon seeing the pandas. According to his recollection, on the second day of her arrival in China, Mrs. Nixon eagerly visited the Beijing Zoo, where, despite having a dedicated photography team following her, she personally took photos of the pandas, fed them, and bid farewell with reluctance, continuously praising their cuteness and tentatively expressing her desire to obtain pandas.

During a shopping trip, Mrs. Nixon and her entourage purchased a large number of panda-themed toys. Tang Longbin sensed that this was a deliberate attempt to win over the pandas. He later reported this to Premier Zhou, who at the time didn't make any explicit remarks.

In fact, as early as 1956-1957, both the Rare Bird Farm in Miami, Florida, and the Chicago Zoo in the United States had written to the Beijing Zoo, hoping to "exchange money or animals for a pair of giant pandas from China." However, due to the limited number of female pandas at the Beijing Zoo—two of which were already earmarked for the Soviet Union—and the prevailing tensions of the Cold War era between China and the United States, coupled with opposition from the U.S. State Department, the exchange plans fell through.

**Premier Zhou's Decision: Gifting Two Pandas to the United States**

President Nixon hoped to seize the opportunity of his visit to China to once again pursue the chance of obtaining pandas. During the visit, as per international custom, both countries exchanged gifts. Nixon presented a set of porcelain swans crafted by the renowned American ceramist Edward Marshall Boehm, as well as crystal glass vases. China reciprocated with double-sided Su embroidery and vases. Nixon, who thought the panda plan had been shelved, was pleasantly surprised to learn during the farewell banquet that China had agreed to gift two giant pandas to the United States.

**Premier Zhou Enlai hosts President Nixon at a banquet, with company of Vice Premier Zhang Chunqiao (right, ousted by the Chinese Communist Party in 1976 and imprisoned serving a lifetime sentence since then till death in 2005).**

There was an amusing detail in the midst of this. Premier Zhou, pointing to the "Panda" brand cigarettes on the table, said to Mrs. Nixon, "We want to give you two of those." Assuming he meant to give her cigarettes, she repeatedly refused, saying, "Cigarettes? I don't smoke..." Premier Zhou smiled and clarified, "Not cigarettes. I mean giant pandas. We want to give you two giant pandas." Mrs. Nixon, delighted, picked up a pack of exquisite cigarettes, pointing to the panda illustration on the cigarette box, and exclaimed to President Nixon, "Hey, Richard, Premier Zhou says they're giving us two giant pandas! Real pandas!"

**Selecting Pandas for the US: Beauty Picking**

China began the rigorous selection process for pandas destined for the United States. Four basic criteria were used for selection: around 3 years of age, good health, moderate size, and attractive appearance. Among these, the criterion of "attractive appearance" was the most difficult to determine. A "beautiful" panda should have small dark eye patches, forming two short figure-eights, with moderate ear black patches, clear black-and-white boundaries, a round head, moderate length of mouth, and a robust physique.

After comparing pandas from the Beijing Zoo and other locations like Wolong and Baoxing in Sichuan Province, two pandas, Ling-Ling (female) and Hsing-Hsing (male), who had lived at the Beijing Zoo for less than a year, were selected. Before departing, the two pandas received special treatment, enjoying a diet of milk, eggs, and vitamins, items that were difficult for ordinary people to obtain in China at that time.

**Selection of pandas gifted to the United States in 1972 was a nationwide beauty-picking event**

## 1972 Became the "Panda Year" in the US

Two months after Nixon's visit to China, Ling-Ling and Hsing-Hsing arrived at the Washington Zoo, where they were welcomed by over 8,000 American citizens, braving the rain. Mrs. Nixon also personally attended the unveiling ceremony of the panda pavilion at the zoo. On the first day the pandas were publicly displayed, 20,000 people queued up to see them, causing traffic jams.

Americans were fascinated by Ling-Ling and Hsing-Hsing, sparking a panda craze across the country. Every move of the pandas became the focus of media attention, and panda-themed products such as beer bottles and picture books flooded the market. Even the green wicker crates labeled "People's Republic of China," which were used to transport them to the US, were put on display. Consequently, 1972 was dubbed the "Panda Year" by the American public.

**Illustration of arrival of Ling-Ling and Hsing-Hsing in Washington D. C. in 1972 welcomed by a huge crowd of people braving a heavy rain**

### Zoo Advertises: Soliciting Fresh Bamboo

However, the Washington Zoo soon encountered a tricky problem: how to meet the massive demand for bamboo from Ling-Ling and Hsing-Hsing. Bamboo constitutes 99% of a panda's diet, and without it, they cannot survive. These pandas were particularly picky about the quality of bamboo; they wouldn't touch it if it wasn't fresh. The zoo had to publish advertisements soliciting fresh bamboo from the public.

A girl named Nancy Tuffs saw the advertisement and called the zoo. Her parents were both China enthusiasts, and they had over 2 acres of bamboo in their yard. Zoo staff were delighted after inspecting the Tuffs' bamboo grove, as they found it to be the exact type of bamboo the pandas preferred. The Tuffs family became the supplier of bamboo for the Washington Zoo, with hundreds of pounds of bamboo being cut down from their property every week, exclusively for Ling-Ling and Hsing-Hsing.

**Nancy's bamboo backyard**

## Panda Ambassadors Through Five US Presidencies

Ling-Ling gave birth to cubs four times, but all of them died. During this time, the Washington Zoo tried everything to help her, even borrowing a male panda from the London Zoo for mating, but without success. In 1992, Ling-Ling died unexpectedly in her cage due to heart disease, at the age of 23. For a panda to reach 20 years old means it has entered old age, equivalent to 80 to 90 years old in human terms. In 1997, the National Zoo erected a monument for Ling-Ling, stating, "The giant panda of our country is a gift from the People's Republic of China, bringing joy to millions of visitors."

Seven years later, at the age of 28, Hsing-Hsing also succumbed to organ failure due to old age. The zoo, unable to see it suffer, euthanized it. It is said that before Hsing-Hsing passed away, it had a good appetite, enjoying sweet potatoes, bamboo shoots, rice porridge, and its favorite Starbucks blueberry muffins. With that, Ling-Ling and Hsing-Hsing completed their special mission of over 20 years. They served through the administrations of five US presidents—Nixon, Ford, Carter, Reagan, and George H.W. Bush—making indelible contributions to the development of Sino-US relations.

**Ling-Ling and Hsing-Hsing in the National Zoo in Washington DC courtesy of the Smithsonian Institutes**

# Roles of Pandas Told in Chinese Media

In this section, we retell and summarize what were reported and described in numerous popular Chinese media over time about roles of pandas in the world. Here we go.

Wild giant pandas worldwide number about 1590, with just over 200 in captivity. Due to their low reproductive rates and high requirements for living environments, giant pandas have always been labeled as endangered animals. Their rarity, uniqueness, adorable appearance, and non-aggressive nature make giant pandas inherently possess the qualities of "friendly ambassadors."

**Role One: Diplomacy and Peace Envoy**

In modern times, pandas have been gifted for political purposes. In 1941, Chiang Kai-shek, the Soong sisters, and many senior officials of the Kuomintang (Chinese Nationalist Party) officially donated a pair of pandas to the United States Relief and Rehabilitation Administration for China. In the 1950s, China initiated "panda diplomacy," presenting pandas as state gifts on behalf of the government and people to countries or regions with which China maintained good relations or hoped to establish relations. Nine countries, including the Soviet Union, North Korea, the United States, the United Kingdom, France, Germany, Japan, Spain, and Mexico, received 23 pandas from China. The peak of "panda diplomacy" was reached when President Nixon received pandas during his 1972 visit to China.

These panda ambassadors received "head of state treatment" in the recipient countries. When Ling-Ling, a panda living in the United States, lost one of her cubs, the World Wildlife Fund even lowered its flag to half-mast for the first time. In 1982, in response to the global call for endangered species protection, China stopped the practice of giving giant pandas to foreign countries for free, marking the end of the era when pandas were given as "state gifts." Politically significant gifts were limited to domestic purposes (meaning such gifts are limited to Taiwan and Hong Kong).

**Role Two: Commercial Counselor**

However, the international journey of giant pandas did not end there. In 1984, the Chinese government proposed a panda leasing program, allowing countries interested in obtaining pandas to rent them for short-term exhibitions at local zoos for a fee. Pandas transformed from "peace envoys" to "commercial counselors." Prior to the 1984 Los Angeles Olympics, China leased a pair of pandas, Yong Yong and Yin Xin, from the Beijing Zoo to the United States for a three-month exhibition, generating millions of dollars in ticket revenue for American zoos in just a few months. Subsequently, pandas toured Canada, Ireland, Sweden, Belgium, and other countries.

However, the heavy influx of visitors each day delayed panda breeding. To attract visitors, some zoos even trained pandas to perform acrobatics. In the early 1990s, an increasing number of environmental protection groups began to oppose panda leasing. Panda exhibitions came to an end as a result. According to the 1975 Convention on International Trade in Endangered Species of Wild Fauna and Flora, foreign zoos could only obtain pandas through leasing, under the guise of scientific research exchange.

**Illustration of a panda performing acrobatics**

Therefore, after two years of negotiation between the China Wildlife Conservation Association, the China Zoo Association, and international animal protection organizations, an agreement was reached to conduct cooperative research with foreign countries. Foreign zoos could lease giant pandas from China for collaborative research. The leasing period for a pair of sub-adult giant pandas typically would last 10 years, with the lessee zoo paying $1 million in annual lease fees. If pandas give birth during the lease period, the average annual rent would increase by $600,000, and the offspring would have to be returned to China after two years. If a panda dies, its body also would have to be returned to

China. Chinese experts could take turns with foreign counterparts to conduct research on giant pandas, and foreign zoos would have to pay $10 million in cooperation fees for a 10-year collaboration.

In 1994, for example, two pandas from the Chengdu Research Base of Giant Panda Breeding, served as "scientific exchange ambassadors," were sent to the Shirahama Wildlife Park in Japan. Since then, many zoos in Japan, including those in Wakayama and Seoul, as well as in the United States, Atlanta, Washington, and Memphis, have begun long-term cooperative research with China. This cooperative approach is more abundant in manpower and material resources, facilitating more comprehensive research on giant pandas. Given the special status of giant pandas both domestically and internationally, their political and diplomatic roles still exist today, such as participating in short-term overseas activities.

# Loaning Pandas to Various Zoos of Note

The history of pandas as gifts and loans is intertwined with diplomatic relations, conservation efforts, and cultural exchange between China and other countries. Here's an overview as a clarification of the issue regarding gifts and loans:

**Early diplomatic gifts**: Pandas have been gifted by China to other countries as a symbol of goodwill and diplomacy for centuries. One of the earliest instances dates back to the Tang Dynasty (618–907 AD), when pandas were given to neighboring countries as diplomatic gifts.

**1950s-1960s**: China resumed its practice of gifting pandas to foreign countries in the 1950s and 1960s. These pandas were typically sent to countries with which China had friendly relations or sought to establish diplomatic ties.

**1970s**: The 1970s marked a significant shift in China's approach to panda diplomacy. Instead of outright gifting pandas, China began loaning pandas to foreign countries, particularly to prominent zoos and wildlife conservation organizations. This allowed China to retain ownership of the pandas while still promoting cultural exchange and raising awareness about panda conservation.

**1972**: It should be emphasized that, although China began loaning pandas to foreign countries in 1970s, the pandas Ling-Ling and Hsing-Hsing, gifted to the United States in 1972 following President Richard Nixon's historic visit to China, were indeed real gifts from China, not loans. That is, unlike panda loans, which involve temporary agreements for the loan of pandas to other countries with strict conditions and terms, the pandas given to the United States in 1972 were considered outright gifts. As such, the National Zoo became the permanent home for Ling-Ling and Hsing-Hsing, where they lived out their lives as cherished ambassadors for their species.

**1980s-1990s**: Throughout the 1980s and 1990s, China continued to loan pandas to countries around the world as part of conservation and breeding programs. These loan agreements often included provisions for research, education, and public outreach aimed at raising awareness about panda conservation and promoting international cooperation.

**2000s-Present**: In recent years, panda loans have become increasingly common, with pandas being loaned to countries in Europe, Asia, North America, and beyond. These loan agreements typically involve strict conservation protocols and long-term commitments to panda care, research, and breeding programs.

Overall, the history of pandas as gifts and loans reflects the evolving nature of international relations, conservation efforts, and cultural diplomacy. While pandas continue to serve as symbols of friendship and cooperation between nations, their conservation remains a top priority for China and the global community, ensuring that these iconic animals will be cherished and protected for generations to come.

Here are some of the most notable panda loans in modern history.

**Zoo Atlanta**, located in Atlanta, Georgia, has played a significant role in panda conservation efforts and has been a key player in the preservation of this iconic species. The zoo's involvement with pandas began in 1999 when it became home to a pair of giant pandas, Lun Lun and Yang Yang, on a long-term loan from China.

Lun Lun, the female panda, and Yang Yang, the male panda, quickly became beloved attractions at Zoo Atlanta, drawing visitors from across the country to witness these rare and majestic animals up close. The pandas' playful antics and charming personalities captured the hearts of zoo visitors and sparked widespread interest in panda conservation.

Zoo Atlanta's collaboration with China extended beyond simply housing the pandas. The zoo actively participated in a collaborative breeding program aimed at increasing the captive panda population and promoting genetic diversity within the species. This breeding program was crucial for the long-term survival of giant pandas, which are classified as endangered due to habitat loss and other threats.

Over the years, Lun Lun and Yang Yang successfully produced several offspring, furthering the zoo's contribution to panda conservation efforts. Their offspring, including Mei Lan, Xi Lan, Po, and Mei Lun and Mei Huan (the first surviving pair of giant panda twins born in the United States), became ambassadors for their species, helping to raise awareness about the plight of pandas in the wild and the importance of conservation.

Zoo Atlanta's partnership with China in the breeding and care of giant pandas exemplifies the collaborative approach taken by zoos and conservation organizations worldwide to protect endangered species and preserve biodiversity. Through education, research, and public outreach efforts, Zoo Atlanta continues to make a significant impact on the conservation of giant pandas and other wildlife species, ensuring a brighter future for these magnificent animals.

**San Diego Zoo**, located in San Diego, California, is renowned for its commitment to wildlife conservation and its extensive collection of rare and endangered species. The zoo's involvement with pandas dates back several decades and has been instrumental in raising awareness about panda conservation and supporting efforts to protect this iconic species.

San Diego Zoo's first involvement with pandas began in the 1980s when it hosted a pair of giant pandas, Bai Yun and Shi Shi, on loan from China. Bai Yun, the female panda, and Shi Shi, the male panda, became popular attractions at the zoo, drawing visitors from around the world to see these rare and captivating animals.

San Diego Zoo's partnership with China extended beyond simply housing pandas. The zoo actively participated in conservation efforts aimed at preserving giant panda populations in the wild and promoting sustainable habitat management practices. This included funding research projects in China, supporting conservation initiatives, and collaborating with Chinese authorities to develop strategies for panda conservation.

In addition to Bai Yun and Shi Shi, San Diego Zoo has also hosted other pandas over the years, including Gao Gao, a male panda who arrived at the zoo in 2003. These pandas played a vital role in raising awareness about the plight of pandas in the wild and the importance of conservation efforts to protect their natural habitat.

San Diego Zoo's involvement with pandas reflects its broader commitment to wildlife conservation and its mission to inspire people to care for and protect the natural world. Through educational programs, research initiatives, and public outreach efforts, the zoo continues to engage visitors and promote conservation awareness, ensuring a brighter future for giant pandas and other endangered species.

**Memphis Zoo**, located in Memphis, Tennessee, has been involved in panda conservation efforts and has had pandas as part of its collection, albeit for a limited time compared to other institutions. The zoo's participation in panda conservation reflects its commitment to wildlife preservation and its role in raising awareness about endangered species.

In 2003, Memphis Zoo welcomed a pair of giant pandas, Le Le and Ya Ya, on loan from China. Le Le, the male panda, and Ya Ya, the female panda, were part of a cooperative agreement between Memphis Zoo and Chinese authorities aimed at promoting panda conservation and public education.

During their time at Memphis Zoo, Le Le and Ya Ya became popular attractions, drawing visitors from across the region to see these rare and majestic animals. The pandas' presence at the zoo provided a unique opportunity for visitors to learn about panda biology, behavior, and the challenges facing wild panda populations.

In addition to serving as ambassadors for their species, Le Le and Ya Ya also participated in breeding programs aimed at increasing the captive panda population and promoting genetic diversity within the species. Although no offspring were produced during their time at Memphis Zoo, their presence contributed to broader conservation efforts aimed at ensuring the long-term survival of giant pandas.

While Le Le and Ya Ya eventually returned to China as part of the terms of their loan agreement, their tenure at Memphis Zoo left a lasting impact on visitors and staff alike. The zoo continues to be actively involved in panda conservation and supports efforts to protect pandas and their habitat in the wild.

Through educational programs, research initiatives, and public outreach efforts, Memphis Zoo remains committed to raising awareness about panda conservation and inspiring conservation action to safeguard these iconic animals for future generations.

**In London**: The zoo in London that hosted pandas is the Zoological Society of London (ZSL) London Zoo, or simply London Zoo. However, it is important to note that pandas were not permanently hosted at London Zoo but were part of temporary exhibits or visits.

For example, in April 1974, two pandas, Chia-Chia and Ching-Ching, were loaned to London Zoo by China for a three-month stay. This marked the first time pandas had been seen in the UK since the 1930s. The pandas were immensely popular, drawing large crowds of visitors eager to catch a glimpse of these rare and iconic animals.

Similarly, in 1991, London Zoo hosted another pair of pandas, Ming-Ming and Bao-Bao, as part of a temporary exhibit called "Panda-mania." The exhibit aimed to raise awareness about panda conservation and the importance of protecting endangered species.

While pandas have made occasional appearances at London Zoo over the years, they have not been permanent residents. These visits have provided valuable opportunities for education and public engagement regarding panda conservation and the broader issue of wildlife conservation.

**In Paris**: The zoo in Paris that hosted pandas is the Zoological Park of Paris, commonly known as Parc Zoologique de Paris or Zoo de Vincennes. The zoo is located in the Bois de Vincennes, in the 12th arrondissement of Paris, France.

In January 2012, two giant pandas, a male named Yuan Zi and a female named Huan Huan, arrived at the Zoo de Vincennes on a 10-year loan from China. This marked the first time in over two decades that pandas had been hosted in France. The pandas were a diplomatic gift from China to France, symbolizing the strengthening of relations between the two countries.

The arrival of Yuan Zi and Huan Huan at Zoo de Vincennes generated significant excitement and public interest. The pandas quickly became star attractions, drawing large crowds of visitors eager to see these rare and beloved animals up close.

Zoo de Vincennes created a special habitat for the pandas, featuring lush bamboo forests, rocky outcrops, and pools for swimming and cooling off. Visitors to the zoo had the opportunity to observe the pandas as they foraged for bamboo, played, and interacted with each other.

Yuan Zi and Huan Huan's stay at Zoo de Vincennes was part of a broader conservation and breeding program aimed at increasing the captive panda population and promoting genetic diversity within the species. The pandas' presence at the zoo also provided valuable opportunities for education and public outreach regarding panda conservation and the importance of protecting endangered species.

In August 2021, Huan Huan gave birth to twin pandas, which was a significant milestone for Zoo de Vincennes and panda conservation efforts worldwide. The birth of the twin pandas was celebrated as a testament to the success of the breeding program and the dedication of the staff at the zoo.

Overall, the hosting of pandas at Zoo de Vincennes in Paris was a memorable and highly successful endeavor, highlighting the importance of international cooperation in wildlife conservation and the power of these iconic animals to inspire and captivate people around the world.

**In Berlin:** In June 2017, two giant pandas named Meng Meng and Jiao Qing arrived at Zoo Berlin on loan from China. Their arrival marked a significant event for the zoo and for Berlin as a whole. The pandas were officially unveiled to the public in July 2017, and they quickly became one of the zoo's main attractions, drawing large crowds of visitors.

Meng Meng and Jiao Qing's presence at Zoo Berlin was part of a 15-year agreement between China and Germany, with the aim of promoting panda conservation, research, and cultural exchange. The pandas' enclosure at Zoo Berlin was specially designed to mimic their natural habitat as closely as possible. It features lush vegetation, climbing structures, and areas for both indoor and outdoor exploration. Visitors to the zoo can observe the pandas from various vantage points, including viewing platforms and glass viewing windows.

Meng Meng is a female panda born on July 10, 2013, in the Chengdu Research Base of Giant Panda Breeding in China. Her name means "dream" in Chinese. She is known for her playful and curious nature, often seen climbing trees and exploring her enclosure. Jiao Qing is a male panda born on July 15, 2010, also at the Chengdu Research Base of Giant Panda Breeding. His name means "darling" or "darling boy" in Chinese. Jiao Qing is known for his more laid-back demeanor compared to Meng Meng, but he also enjoys engaging in enrichment activities and interacting with his keepers.

The arrival of Meng Meng and Jiao Qing generated a great deal of excitement and media attention in Germany, highlighting the importance of international cooperation in wildlife conservation. The pandas continue to be beloved by visitors to Zoo Berlin and serve as ambassadors for their species, raising awareness about the plight of giant pandas in the wild and the need for conservation efforts to protect them.

One of the goals of hosting giant pandas at Zoo Berlin is to contribute to international breeding efforts aimed at increasing the captive population and ultimately supporting the long-term survival of the species. While Meng Meng and Jiao Qing have not yet produced offspring, the zoo remains hopeful for future breeding success.

**In Tokyo**: The zoo in Tokyo that hosted pandas is the Ueno Zoological Gardens, commonly known as Ueno Zoo. Located in Ueno Park, Taito, Tokyo, Japan, Ueno Zoo has been home to giant pandas for several decades.

Ueno Zoo has a long history of hosting pandas, beginning in 1972 when the Chinese government gifted a pair of giant pandas, Ling-Ling and Kan-Kan, to Japan as a symbol of goodwill and friendship between the two countries. Ling-Ling and Kan-Kan quickly became beloved attractions at Ueno Zoo, drawing visitors from across Japan and around the world.

In subsequent years, Ueno Zoo continued to host pandas as part of its collection, contributing to panda conservation efforts and promoting public awareness about the plight of this endangered species. The zoo has been actively involved in breeding programs aimed at increasing the captive panda population and preserving genetic diversity within the species.

Over the years, several pandas have resided at Ueno Zoo, delighting visitors with their playful antics and charming personalities. The pandas' presence at the zoo has played a significant role in raising awareness about panda conservation and the importance of protecting endangered species.

As of my last update in January 2022, Ueno Zoo continues to host pandas, with the current residents being Shin Shin (female) and Ri Ri (male), who arrived at the zoo in 2011 on a 10-year loan from China. The birth of several panda cubs at Ueno Zoo in recent years, including twins in 2020, has been celebrated as a testament to the success of the zoo's breeding program and the dedication of its staff.

**In South Korea**: The zoo in South Korea that hosted pandas is Seoul Grand Park Zoo, which is located in Gwacheon, a city just south of Seoul, South Korea.

In 1994, South Korea received two giant pandas, a male named Tong Tong and a female named Yu Yu, on a 10-year loan from China. The pandas were hosted at Seoul Grand Park Zoo as part of a diplomatic agreement between China and South Korea.

Tong Tong and Yu Yu quickly became popular attractions at Seoul Grand Park Zoo, drawing visitors from across South Korea to see these rare and beloved animals. The pandas' presence at the zoo contributed to public awareness about panda conservation and the importance of protecting endangered species.

Following the end of the initial 10-year loan period, Tong Tong and Yu Yu were returned to China in 2004. Since then, there have been no pandas permanently hosted at Seoul Grand Park Zoo.

It's worth noting that while Seoul Grand Park Zoo hosted pandas temporarily, South Korea has not been a regular host of pandas compared to other countries like China, Japan, and the United States. However, the pandas' stay at the zoo left a lasting impression on visitors and contributed to broader efforts to raise awareness about wildlife conservation in South Korea.

**In Taiwan**: The zoo in Taiwan that hosted pandas is Taipei Zoo, located in Taipei, Taiwan. Taipei Zoo has been home to giant pandas as part of a cooperative agreement with China.

In December 2008, Taiwan received two giant pandas, a male named Tuan Tuan and a female named Yuan Yuan, on loan from China. The pandas were a gift from China to Taiwan as a symbol of goodwill and friendship between the two sides of the Taiwan Strait. The names "Tuan Tuan" and "Yuan Yuan" together form a phrase that means "reunion" or "reuniting" in Mandarin, reflecting the hope for improved cross-strait relations.

Tuan Tuan and Yuan Yuan quickly became star attractions at Taipei Zoo, drawing large crowds of visitors eager to see these rare and beloved animals. The pandas' presence at the zoo contributed to public awareness about panda conservation and the importance of protecting endangered species.

In 2013, Tuan Tuan and Yuan Yuan successfully produced a cub, named Yuan Zai, through natural mating. Yuan Zai's birth was celebrated as a significant milestone for panda conservation efforts and the success of the breeding program at Taipei Zoo.

Since then, Tuan Tuan and Yuan Yuan have remained at Taipei Zoo, where they continue to be popular attractions and ambassadors for wildlife conservation. Their presence has helped to foster closer ties between Taiwan and China and has contributed to efforts to promote understanding and cooperation across the Taiwan Strait.

**In Hong Kong**: The zoo in Hong Kong that hosted pandas is Ocean Park Hong Kong, a theme park and marine mammal park located in Wong Chuk Hang and Nam Long Shan, in the Southern District of Hong Kong.

Ocean Park Hong Kong has been home to giant pandas as part of a collaborative agreement with China. In 1999, the park received a pair of giant pandas, a male named An An and a female named Jia Jia, on loan from China. The pandas were initially housed in the Giant Panda Habitat at the park, which was specially designed to mimic their natural habitat and provide for their welfare.

An An and Jia Jia quickly became popular attractions at Ocean Park Hong Kong, drawing visitors from around the world to see these rare and beloved animals. The pandas' presence at the park contributed to public awareness about panda conservation and the importance of protecting endangered species.

In 2012, An An and Jia Jia successfully produced a cub, named Le Le, through natural mating. Le Le's birth was celebrated as a significant milestone for panda conservation efforts and the success of the breeding program at Ocean Park Hong Kong.

Jia Jia, the female panda, passed away in October 2016 at the age of 38, making her one of the oldest pandas in captivity at the time. An An, the male panda, continued to reside at Ocean Park Hong Kong until his passing in 2020.

Ocean Park Hong Kong's hosting of pandas has been an important aspect of its conservation and education efforts, helping to raise awareness about panda conservation and promote understanding of these iconic animals among visitors to the park.

# Events of Diplomatic Recalls of Pandas

Diplomatic recalls of pandas are the events that have occurred in the past due to various political, diplomatic, or conservation-related reasons. While pandas are often used as symbols of friendship and goodwill between nations, their loan agreements are subject to diplomatic considerations and occasional recalls. Below are some notable instances in chronical order.

**2001**: In April 2001, a collision occurred between a U.S. Navy EP-3 surveillance plane and a Chinese fighter jet over the South China Sea, near Hainan Island. The U.S. plane was forced to make an emergency landing on Hainan Island, where the crew was detained by Chinese authorities for 11 days. This incident strained relations between China and the United States, leading to a diplomatic standoff.

As a response to the incident and the ensuing diplomatic tensions, China decided to recall two giant pandas, Mei Xiang and Tian Tian, from the Smithsonian's National Zoo in Washington, D.C. Mei Xiang and Tian Tian had been on loan to the National Zoo since their arrival in 2000 as part of a collaborative agreement between China and the United States aimed at promoting panda conservation and research.

The recall of Mei Xiang and Tian Tian was widely viewed as a diplomatic gesture by China, symbolizing its displeasure with the United States and the strained state of bilateral relations at the time. The decision to recall the pandas was seen as a symbolic move to express China's dissatisfaction with the U.S. government's handling of the EP-3 incident and to exert diplomatic pressure on the United States.

The recall of Mei Xiang and Tian Tian generated significant media attention and public discussion, highlighting the unique role that pandas play in international diplomacy. The pandas' departure from the National Zoo was met with disappointment by zoo staff and visitors alike, who had grown fond of Mei Xiang and Tian Tian during their time at the zoo.

Following the resolution of the diplomatic standoff and the release of the crew members, efforts were made to repair and normalize relations between China and the United States. Mei Xiang and Tian Tian eventually returned to the National Zoo in December 2001, marking the end of their temporary recall and the resumption of the panda loan agreement between the two countries.

**2008**: In 2008, China recalled pandas from several U.S. zoos as a response to the political situation and diplomatic tensions surrounding the protests in Tibet and the controversy surrounding the Beijing Olympics. The unrest in Tibet and international criticism of China's human rights record ahead of the Beijing Olympics led to strained relations between China and Western countries, including the United States.

The pandas, which were on loan to U.S. zoos as part of conservation and breeding programs aimed at preserving the endangered species and promoting international cooperation in wildlife conservation, were temporarily returned to China until diplomatic tensions eased.

One of the notable instances of panda recalls during this period involved the pair of giant pandas, Mei Xiang and Tian Tian, who resided at the Smithsonian's National Zoo in Washington, D.C. Mei Xiang and Tian Tian had been living at the National Zoo since their arrival in 2000 and had become beloved attractions and symbols of the close relationship between China and the United States.

The temporary recall of Mei Xiang and Tian Tian, along with other pandas hosted at U.S. zoos, was seen as a diplomatic gesture by China to express its dissatisfaction with the political situation and diplomatic tensions at the time. The recall of the pandas received significant media attention and was widely interpreted as a response to the strained relations between China and Western countries, particularly the United States.

The pandas were eventually returned to their respective zoos in the United States once diplomatic tensions eased and the political situation stabilized. The episode highlighted the unique role that pandas play in international diplomacy and the delicate balance between political considerations and conservation efforts in panda loan agreements between China and other countries.

**2010:** In 2010, relations between China and Japan became strained due to a territorial dispute over the Senkaku/Diaoyu Islands in the East China Sea. The long-standing dispute over the sovereignty of these uninhabited islands intensified following Japan's decision to detain a Chinese fishing boat captain near the disputed waters.

The escalation of tensions between China and Japan prompted China to recall two giant pandas, named Kang Kang and Lan Lan, from Japan. Kang Kang and Lan Lan had been on loan to Japan since 2000 and had been residing at the Adventure World Zoo in Shirahama, Wakayama Prefecture, as part of a diplomatic agreement aimed at promoting friendship and cultural exchange between the two countries.

The recall of Kang Kang and Lan Lan was widely interpreted as a diplomatic gesture by China in response to the escalating tensions and deteriorating relations between China and Japan at the time. The decision to recall the pandas was seen as a symbolic move to express China's dissatisfaction with Japan's actions and to exert diplomatic pressure on the Japanese government to resolve the territorial dispute.

The recall of Kang Kang and Lan Lan received significant media attention and sparked public discussion about the role of pandas in international diplomacy. The pandas' departure from Japan was met with disappointment by zoo staff and visitors alike, who had grown fond of Kang Kang and Lan Lan during their time at the Adventure World Zoo.

Despite the temporary recall of Kang Kang and Lan Lan, efforts were made to improve and normalize relations between China and Japan in the aftermath of the territorial dispute. The pandas eventually returned to China once diplomatic tensions eased, marking the end of their temporary stay in Japan and the resumption of panda loan agreements between the two countries.

**2020**: In May 2020, China recalled two giant pandas, Tuan Tuan and Yuan Yuan, from Taiwan. Tuan Tuan and Yuan Yuan had been on loan to Taiwan from China since 2008 and were temporarily hosted at Taipei Zoo. The recall of the pandas followed deteriorating relations between China and Taiwan, with China citing political issues as the reason for the recall.

The pandas, whose names together mean "reunion" in Mandarin, were originally gifted to Taiwan by China as a symbol of goodwill and friendship between the two sides of the Taiwan Strait. Their arrival in Taiwan in December 2008 was seen as a significant diplomatic gesture and marked a thaw in cross-strait relations at the time.

Tuan Tuan and Yuan Yuan quickly became popular attractions at Taipei Zoo, drawing large crowds of visitors eager to see these rare and beloved animals. The pandas' presence at the zoo contributed to public awareness about panda conservation and the importance of protecting endangered species.

However, as relations between China and Taiwan became increasingly strained in the years following their arrival, the future of Tuan Tuan and Yuan Yuan in Taiwan became uncertain. In May 2020, China decided to recall the pandas, citing political issues as the reason for their return to mainland China.

The recall of Tuan Tuan and Yuan Yuan generated significant media attention and public discussion in Taiwan, with many expressing sadness over the departure of the beloved pandas. Their return to mainland China marked the end of their more than a decade-long stay in Taiwan and signaled a further deterioration in cross-strait relations.

The recall of Tuan Tuan and Yuan Yuan underscored the complex political dynamics between China and Taiwan and the ways in which animals, particularly pandas, can become entangled in diplomatic disputes and international relations.

# The World as a Whole in Helping Pandas

There are diverse ways in which individuals, communities, and organizations are coming together to help pandas and ensure their survival for future generations. These include volunteer work, habitat restoration, international collaborations, and public awareness campaigns. The efforts to help pandas demonstrate the power of collective action and the importance of conservation efforts in safeguarding endangered species and their habitats.

**Panda conservation volunteers**: Every year, hundreds of volunteers from around the world travel to panda conservation centers in China to contribute their time and expertise to help care for pandas and support conservation efforts. These dedicated volunteers assist with tasks such as cleaning enclosures, preparing food, monitoring panda behavior, and conducting research. Their hard work and commitment play a crucial role in ensuring the well-being and survival of pandas in captivity and in the wild.

**Panda habitat restoration**: In recent years, conservation organizations and local communities in China have undertaken extensive efforts to restore and protect panda habitat in the country's mountainous regions. These initiatives include reforestation projects, establishment of wildlife corridors, and implementation of sustainable land management practices. By restoring degraded habitat and creating safe corridors for pandas to move between fragmented forest patches, these efforts help to expand panda populations and promote genetic diversity.

**International collaborations**: Many countries around the world have partnered with China in collaborative efforts to support panda conservation and research. Through initiatives such as panda breeding programs, scientific research projects, and educational outreach, international collaborations contribute to the global conservation of pandas and their habitat. By sharing knowledge, resources, and expertise, these partnerships help to strengthen conservation efforts and promote greater awareness of the importance of protecting endangered species.

**Public awareness campaigns**: Wildlife conservation organizations, zoos, and educational institutions frequently launch public awareness campaigns to raise awareness about the plight of pandas and the need for conservation action. These campaigns utilize various media platforms, including social media, television, print, and online publications, to reach audiences around the world and inspire them to act to protect pandas and their habitat. By engaging the public and fostering a sense of empathy and responsibility towards pandas, these campaigns help to mobilize support for conservation efforts and drive positive change.

More notably, there is also a world-wide adoption effort involving many different programs.

These programs are initiatives offered by wildlife conservation organizations, zoos, and panda research centers around the world to engage the public in supporting panda conservation efforts, allowing individuals, families, and organizations to symbolically adopt a panda by donating, which helps fund conservation projects, habitat restoration, research, and education programs aimed at protecting pandas and their habitat.

Here are some aspects of these panda adoption programs:

**Symbolic adoption**: Panda adoption programs typically offer participants the opportunity to symbolically "adopt" a panda by donating. In exchange for their support, adopters receive a symbolic adoption certificate, a photo of the adopted panda, and sometimes other perks such as updates on the adopted panda's well-being and conservation activities.

**Education and outreach**: Panda adoption programs often include educational components designed to raise awareness about panda conservation and inspire action to protect these endangered animals. Adopters may receive educational materials about pandas, conservation updates, and opportunities to participate in conservation-themed events, workshops, and activities.

**Partnerships and collaboration**: Many panda adoption programs are run in partnership with wildlife conservation organizations, zoos, and panda research centers in China and around the world. These partnerships enable adopters to support a wide range of conservation initiatives and benefit from the expertise and resources of organizations dedicated to panda conservation.

**Global reach**: Panda adoption programs have a global reach, allowing people from all over the world to participate in panda conservation efforts. Adopters come from diverse backgrounds and countries, united by a shared love for pandas and a desire to make a positive impact on their conservation.

Overall, panda adoption programs provide a meaningful way for individuals and organizations to support panda conservation efforts, contribute to the protection of this endangered species, and play a role in ensuring a brighter future for pandas and their fragile habitats. By participating in these programs, adopters become ambassadors for panda conservation, helping to raise awareness and inspire others to join in the efforts to protect these iconic animals.

# Panda is World's Treasure and Should not be Used as a Political Tool

Pandas, with their endearing black-and-white fur, playful demeanor, and status as a symbol of conservation, hold a special place in the hearts of people around the world. However, amidst their global popularity, there exists a troubling trend of using pandas as political pawns, exploiting their allure for diplomatic leverage. Pandas should be cherished as a global treasure, enjoyed by all, and protected from politicization, regardless of their native habitat in China.

Firstly, pandas are more than just charismatic creatures; they represent a shared responsibility to conserve biodiversity and protect endangered species. As inhabitants of bamboo forests in China, pandas play a crucial role in maintaining the health of their ecosystem. Their conservation status serves as a barometer for the overall health of the environment, making their protection a global priority. Therefore, it is imperative that pandas are not used as tools of political negotiation or as rewards in diplomatic exchanges.

Secondly, the enjoyment of pandas should be a universal right, transcending political boundaries and cultural differences. Whether it's through visits to zoos, participation in panda adoption programs, or watching documentaries, people from all walks of life should have the opportunity to experience the wonder of pandas. By fostering a collective appreciation for these majestic creatures, we can inspire greater empathy for nature and a shared commitment to conservation.

Lastly, the fact that pandas are native to China does not grant the country exclusive ownership or control over their fate. While China rightfully plays a central role in panda conservation efforts, it should do so with transparency, collaboration, and a commitment to global stewardship. Exploiting people's love for pandas for political gain undermines the spirit of cooperation and mutual respect that is essential for effective conservation efforts.

# A Panda's Plea: Let Love Prevail

As a panda living in the bamboo forests of China, I have observed with dismay the unfortunate tendency of humans to exploit my species for political gain. It pains me deeply to see my fellow pandas being used as diplomatic tools, traded between nations as bargaining chips in geopolitical games. Therefore, I feel compelled to speak out and express my earnest desire for a world where love and compassion prevail over politics.

My dear human friends, I implore you to see me not as a symbol of power or prestige, but as a living, breathing being deserving of love, respect, and protection. My black-and-white fur may be adorable, and my playful antics may bring joy to your hearts, but I am more than just a cute face. I am a sentient being with thoughts, feelings, and a deep longing for connection with all living creatures.

I long to roam freely in the bamboo forests, to frolic in the sunshine, and to feast on tender bamboo shoots without the burden of geopolitical tensions weighing on my mind. I want to share moments of laughter and camaraderie with humans of all backgrounds, without the shadow of politics looming over our interactions.

It is true that I am fortunate to call China my home, but that does not mean I belong to China alone. I belong to the world, to every person who has ever marveled at my beauty, felt a spark of joy in my presence, or been moved by my plight as an endangered species. I am a global ambassador for peace, unity, and environmental stewardship, and I ask that you treat me as such.

So please, let us set aside political differences and come together in a spirit of love and cooperation. Let us work hand in hand to protect not only pandas like me, but all creatures great and small, and the precious habitats that sustain life on this planet. Together, we can create a world where pandas are cherished for who we are, not for the political agendas we may represent.

With love and hope,
Your Panda Friend

# Afterword

The history of pandas from China as diplomatic gifts reflects the complex interplay between geopolitics and conservation efforts over time. Pandas have been utilized as symbols of goodwill and diplomatic gestures between nations, with their loan agreements often influenced by prevailing political climates. While pandas have undoubtedly served as powerful tools for fostering international relations and promoting cultural exchange, their status as diplomatic gifts has also been subject to fluctuations in political tensions and diplomatic relations between China and recipient countries. This dynamic history underscores the importance of balancing conservation goals with diplomatic considerations and highlights the need for greater cooperation and transparency in panda conservation efforts on a global scale.

This small book results from an effort elaborating on the historical moments and events in the global picture of contemporary world affairs. Through exploring the intricate relationship between pandas, China, and the world, we have peeled back the layers of panda diplomacy to reveal its complexities and nuances. From the earliest instances of panda gifting to the modern era of panda loans and conservation initiatives, each chapter has shed light on the pivotal role that pandas have played in shaping diplomatic relations and promoting international cooperation.

As we reflect on the journey we've taken through the ups and downs of panda diplomacy, it's clear that these beloved creatures hold a special place not only in the hearts of people around the world but also in the annals of history. Their iconic black-and-white fur has become a symbol of unity and peace, transcending borders and political divides to remind us of our shared responsibility to protect and preserve our planet's biodiversity.

Looking ahead, the challenges facing panda conservation are as daunting as ever, but the opportunities for progress are equally abundant. By building upon the lessons of the past and forging new partnerships across borders, we can ensure a brighter future for pandas and all living beings that call our planet home.

After all, pandas are a precious global treasure that should be cherished, protected, and celebrated by all people. They should not be used as political tools or subjected to exploitation based on their native habitat. By recognizing the intrinsic value of pandas and promoting their non-political appreciation, we can uphold their status as symbols of unity, conservation, and hope for future generations.

An overlook of a panda reserve region in southwest China

www.ingramcontent.com/pod-product-compliance
Lightning Source LLC
Chambersburg PA
CBHW021132130726
47988CB00003B/1269